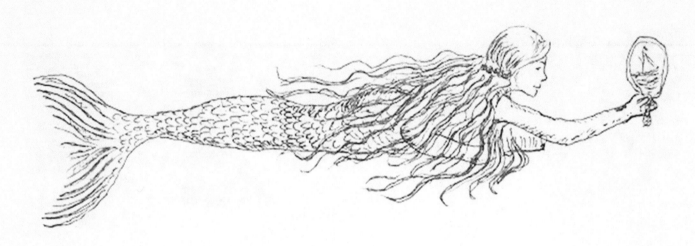

A Mermaid's Reflection

Poetry under the Surface

L E S L I E   L A M P E   L O N G

AuthorHouse™
1663 Liberty Drive
Bloomington, IN 47403
www.authorhouse.com
Phone: 833-262-8899

This book is printed on acid-free paper.

ISBN: 978-1-6655-2698-2 (sc)
978-1-6655-2699-9 (hc)
978-1-6655-2697-5 (e)

Library of Congress Control Number: 2021910478

Print information available on the last page.

Published by AuthorHouse 06/01/2021

authorHOUSE®

When I open my eyes, what do I see?

"Eyes Open" by Leslie Lampe Long

1

Dedication

My dad loved poetry and music,
so we shared the music of poetry
and the poetry of music
throughout my childhood.
It was our way of
deeply knowing
our world and ourselves.
This collection of poems
is dedicated to my dad
and to my mermaid sister, Karen.

Acknowledgments

I have much appreciation for the "COVID Coven," a Zoom group of fellow psychotherapists from across the United States, joined together in mutual support as we adapted our clinical practices to the pandemic in 2020. This remarkably welcoming, encouraging, and open group received me as I discovered myself anew. Thank you to Heather Ferguson, Steven Stern, Stacy Berlin, Julie Oscherwitz Grant, Jane Jordan, Michelle Lalouche-Kadden, Laurel Spindel, and Shaké Topalian for enabling me to reach beyond my comfort zone.

"Far Above" by Leslie Lampe Long

Far Above

The wings of birds,
feathers that
find their way
flying above,
flocking
uncaged,
farsighted,
gaining altitude,
perspective,
distance,
direction.

Looking below,
my flightless self
feathers that ruffle,
opening my cage
alone,
close to grounded.
Hoping to rise
with wings
that find their way
in relation,
to feel it all—
with intimate
perspective.

"Grace" by Leslie Lampe Long

Grace

When the willow
drips
slowly down
her fountain
tears
so
sadly,
I wonder why she's weeping—
if her tears are cleansing,
if her grieving helps her
grow strong.
Her roots hold
as the wayward wind
sprays
her grace.

"Play Interrupted" by Leslie Lampe Long

Thunder Phobia

Mom is terrified,
our play interrupted
suddenly.
We huddle
together
at the window,
in her tight grip.
Together, we answer
the frightful storm—
thrum, thrum!
The drums are
thundering loud,
lightning cymbals flash.
Are we safe now, Mom,
watching this stormy band?
Her tense grip eases;
we exhale.
Can we play now?

"The Bridge between I Am and You Are" by Leslie Lampe Long

The Bridge between I Am and You Are

Our words never quite
connect …
your thoughts and mine.
Perhaps our words are lost,
unable to navigate
the narrows,
moment to
moment
in the fog
of drifting
minds.

And in the drifting,
rising fog
reveals the bridge
between moment and
moment,
between now and
now,
between mind and
body,
between I am
and you are.

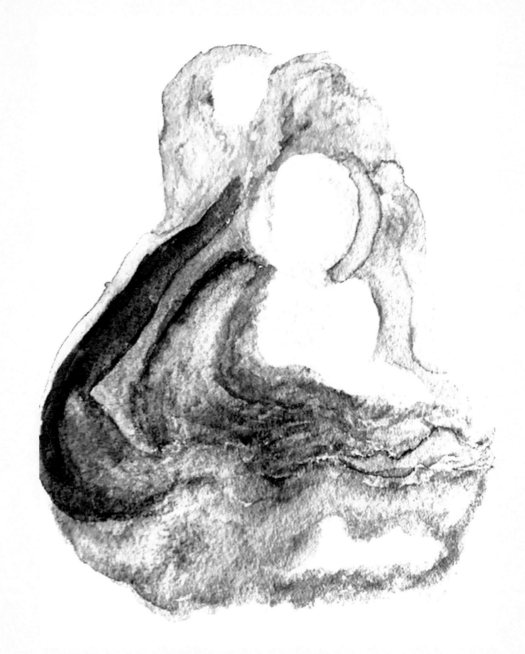

"Why?" by Leslie Lampe Long

Why, God, Why?

Why do you let man
suffer, hate, kill,
unmerciful God?
Do you have an answer?
How can this keep happening?
Can you help us make sense of all of this?
God, are you angry?

We wait for a reply and
hear from close behind us,
"Why, man, why?"

Now, we know it's on us
not to be defined by
hatred or blame,
not to own the sins of others
but to speak out,
to show up,
to find the light,
to be the light
and god on the inside.

When I reach out, who is there?

"Who Is There?" by Leslie Lampe Long

"Late Blooming" by Leslie Lampe Long

Late Bloomer Blues

In my world of fantasy
and not knowing,
hopes pleading,
friends with lovers.
Alone in my room,
music holding me,
late-bloomer blues.

By and by,
a smile, a kiss,
touching mind
and body,
transcending fantasy.
wanting to trust,
but doubt looms.

And the late-blooming flower,
the Montauk daisy,
waits all summer
to bring its strength
and bloom
to the garden.

"Scars" by Leslie Lampe Long

Scars

Days and tears pass,
enduring a time of not knowing
as I try to hide my scars
and tell my story.
I wonder,
do my scars define me?
Can they not haunt,
but give me strength
to overcome regret?
What is the story I will tell?

In and Out

In and out
of my mind
like visions
of past things
and present things
and future,
the thought
of you
in and out.
A web of movement
woven through
strength
of memory,
frailty
of future.

"Entwined" by Leslie Lampe Long

Torn

Searching long,
yielding love so binding,
commitment so soon.
Trying not to disappoint,
but knowing that loving
this way
is tearing me apart
to my very core.
As I crush
from the giving,
my soul searches
for the impossible
soft landing.

Interwoven

The threads
have found themselves
entwined.
At last,
each now
has meaning
for the other,
unraveling past,
extending presence.
Threads receiving
their intimate edge—
interwoven fabric.

"Mermaid Sisters" by Deborah Sosebee

This painting shows the sisters in their 'immortal' just before a spear fisherman emerged between them.

A Mermaid's Reflection

We were immortal then,
my sister and I,
alone by the sea.

Moonlight glimmering,
slipping into dark water
quietly naked,
bathing dreamlike through
the gentle,
reflecting the daytime heat,
a whisper against time,
floating immortal.

Shocked suddenly awake,
our alone shatters—
an emergent mortal,
wild from the deep.

No longer whispers
but fearful calls
as together we escape
to shore,
hiding from moonlight.

Our glimmering immortal,
an echo in our dream.

"Tender Boughs" by Leslie Lampe Long

Tender Boughs

First meeting,
hopeful apprehension
excited tension—
an encounter, a journey?
Wary and wanting
fantasies hold us
that late Fall,
boughs brilliant.

We meet again,
eyes engaging, selves
within our grasp,
committing to journey—
openness,
rootedness,
growing together.
Who are we?
Tender, bare branches.
Awaiting.

We, the fragile,
find ourselves
tumbling into
hollows of
old wounds.
Fantasies splinter,
roots fracture;
without warning,
the bough breaks.

You say I'm Madame Defarge,
knitting your name
beside the guillotine.
On the dark side,
our rootedness ruptures.
Who am I really?
The executioner?

Humbled, holding,
and more knowing,
I claim
my role
in the breaking.

Looking within,
exploring
our wholeness,
we find
our taproot—
wounds and longings,
archaic and fresh.
We emerge to find
our boughs
need tending
and more knowing
for our journey's
deeper possibility …
Spring.

Can I see what others fail to see?

"Outside/Inside" by Leslie Lampe Long

"Drifting" by Leslie Lampe Long

Drifting

Taking to flight,
above the devouring waves.
The sounds of the sea
wash away all others.
Heartfelt longing
to trust the waves,
and the tides
to take me
beneath
the surface safely.
Dwelling
deep within,
beyond thought,
letting go,
safely drifting
along the seabed,
a light shines
from above.
Emerge.
Breathe.

"Life's Marathon" by Leslie Lampe Long

Life's Marathon

Cool wind,
morning mist,
sudden awakening—
am I running toward
or running away?
Longing to become
stronger,
worthy,
without regret,
forgiving,
not forgetting.
This is my time,
my body—
life's marathon,
losing track
of the miles,
the time, the pain.
Feeling the earth
with each step,
I run toward–
to become.

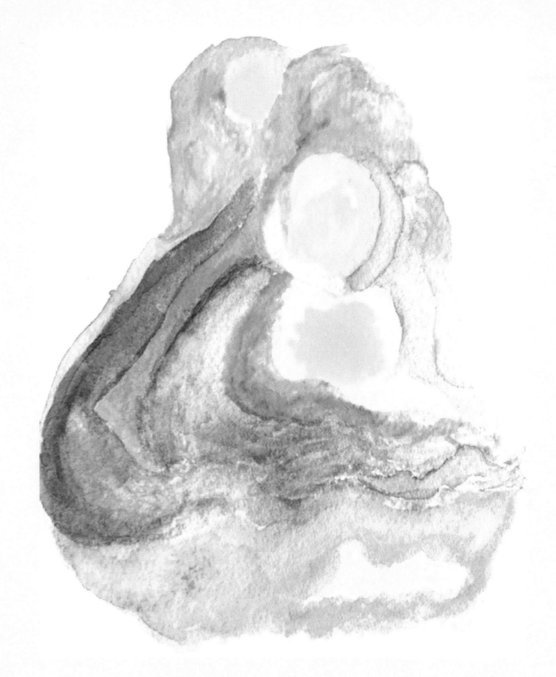

"Belonging" by Leslie Lampe Long

Shadow Self

The ephemeral self,
blind to us.
Emerge from
the dark and hidden
to create what you are.
Feel the energy,
find movement,
own your strength,
and become whole.
We are one,
both the dark
and the light.

Belonging

We find each other
in the mirror,
dear friends—
sharing
our lives' purpose.
Living
through our lives and loves
together,
cherishing intimacy and
connectedness.
As we sing
our songs,
and remember our toasts,
in the joy of belonging,
we dance!

"Spirit Mother" by Leslie Lampe Long

Spirit Mother

dedicated to my stepdaughter, Jessica

Your evanescence
grows with the wind,
flows with the tides,
blows with the sand.
Hold me
for just a moment
in your safe embrace.
Please teach me,
the one without children,
how to create
a family.
Lend me your strength
to nurture, to protect, to hold,
to share, to mirror,
to limit,
to let go,
and together,
just be—
found family.

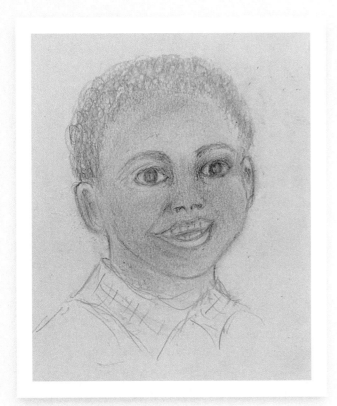 

"Andrew and Amanda" by Leslie Lampe Long

Self Images

Philadelphia Inner City, Fourth Grade

The students watch
in awe:
first photos,
images of their own faces
and selves developing
in our darkroom.
Once portraits of presidents,
now students' portraits.
Their beaming
brown faces
encircle our classroom.

From My Remove

Immersed in Blackness,
but I am not of it,
my own image clouds.
From my remove,
a humbled self,
struck
beyond resounding
with vitality,
powerful essence
down the narrowing alley
of years, resilience.
Beyond words,
borne by a
hunger to understand
the world I cannot know,
my own liberation
bound up with theirs.

WHY ARE YOU HERE?

WHY ARE YOU HERE?

WHY ARE YOU HERE?

WHY ARE YOU?

Boardroom Shame
(Not a PowerPoint Presentation)

"Come to the executive meeting,"
her boss directs.
She enters the meeting,
MEN
looking at her.
"Could someone get us some coffee?"
Not responding, in silence, she takes her seat.
Breaking in, Senior Boss asks her,
"Why are you here?"
Her own boss is mute.
"To share national—"
Interrupting her,
"No need for you to stay," says Senior Boss.
"You can go now."
In silence, she leaves the room.

In the hall, she bursts into
tears of shame.

Boardroom Erotica

In the boardroom:
the executive morning meeting,
all men and her.
"Welcome! So glad you're here.
May we get you some coffee?
And we'd love to get your perspective
on our national strategy."
The men seem careful
not to notice her breasts
underneath her silk blouse.

In the hall, she smiles.

EYES WIDE OPEN

This experience of shame
was to be not a ceiling
but rather
a bridge
for me to cross
and to help
other women cross,
with eyes wide open.

"Conversation" by Leslie Lampe Long

Symphony as Conversation
or
How does the conductor hear
the whole orchestra?

On the challenge of moderating hundreds of Zoom participants
in a multiday online colloquium with Steven Stern, "composer/
conductor," and Heather Ferguson, "first violin"

Prelude
Preparing for dissonance,
imagining harmony

First Movement
Interpreting the score,
hearing the ensemble,
conductor's focus: the solo

Second Movement
Conductor and performers in relation,
call-and-response, mutative exchange,
intonation, rhythmic transitions,
aspiration to balance, timing,
collaboration,
frame

Third Movement
Spotting airlessness and tension,
compensatory adaptation,
integrated spontaneity,
pockets of air, new breath,
shared vulnerability,
the violin's melody dancing

Finale
Surprise tension,
music with eyes that feel,
notes that bridge,
the questions we ask,
knowing what we cannot know

When I open my heart, what do I feel?

all of us
have
things
we
hold dear to our hearts
that
keep
us
rooted
so
that
we
will
not lose
ourselves in
this vast and gloriously messy
ocean of life

A
safe
holding
place
nearby

&
not
drift
far far
away

"Hope" by Leslie Lampe Long

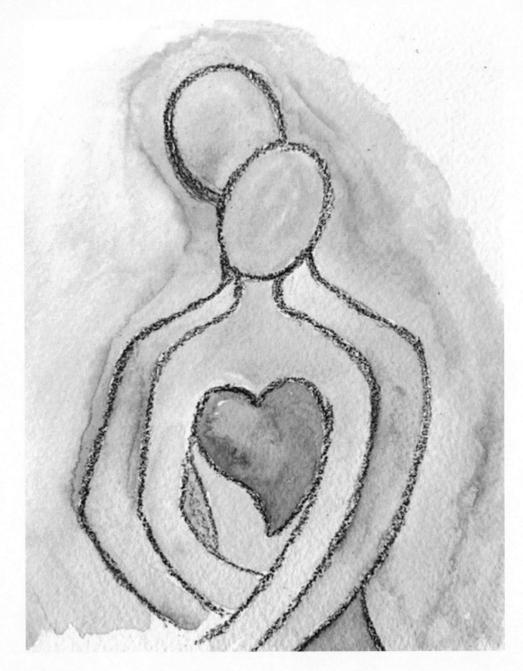

"Wonder" by Leslie Lampe Long

Awakening

Dedicated to my husband on our 20th anniversary

Smiling life
lights the night,
natural love at sunrise.
Imagination, inspiration
tenderly meeting the other.
So eager for life …
strength from within,
the vital sensations
of joining.
The time, the conversation
indescribable
moments.
Could I have lived
without this—
person fulfilling,
our selves meeting?
Perhaps, but an emptiness
would always be.
Don't wonder too much.
All of this so new,
I haven't made a habit
of being
in love–
happiness as intense,
as is my wonder
at new sensitivities–
becoming a
WE,
as I hold onto
ME.

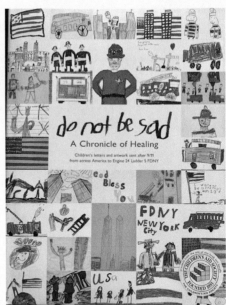

Photos of FDNY Engine 24/Ladder 5 with banners our agency created to thank the community, published in Do Not Be Sad: A Chronicle of Healing, *a collection of children's art sent to 24&5, and Bonnee Sharp with the portraits she painted for the families of the eleven men this firehouse lost on 9/11*

Walking with You, Believing in You

September 11, 2001

The survivors, we
bereft with despair,
an advertising agency
writers, artists, staff,
suddenly devoid of purpose.
Hiding our desperation,
humbly venturing out
to our first responders,
hoping to help
Engine 24, Ladder 5,
traumatized—
eleven of their company gone,
but no loss of their purpose.
How can we help?
We're a neighbor,
just an advertising agency.
The firehouse welcomes
our artists, writers.
and accountants.
Together
we help 24 & 5
thank
the community.
Purpose now shared,
our own healing begins.

May the Road Rise Up

Vinny died a hero
on his fortieth birthday—
climbing 110 flights
to save lives.
His body perished,
remains never found.

Way too soon,
the wake
to celebrate his life.
Together, we
step onto the bus,
taking us to his hometown pub.
He is alive on this bus;
Lieutenant Fun, they call him.
We together–
boisterous,
laughing with Vinny,
as his brothers take turns
imitating
his improv, his Elvis,
his pranks.
Ours is the laughter
of aching souls.
His bereaved family
awaits.

This is how I know Vinny—
on this bus
with his brothers,
as the bagpipes
welcome him home.

"Here and Gone" by Leslie Lampe Long

Here and Gone

Driving her Dad's car for the last time,
driving Dad's car for the first time,
shifting through the gears of Dad's life
and through the gears of her own.

Driving Dad's car for the first time
with him sitting beside her,
teaching her how to shift the gears.
Patient he was—enduring
the stops, the starts, the stalls
of her turbocharged life.

Driving Dad's car for the last time,
with him no longer beside her but here still,
not knowing this would be the last time,
telling her,
"They come and take your car away
when you get old, you know."

Her dad driving her all the first times,
singing his road-trip songs;
when would they get there?
She was in a hurry;
singing made the time fly.

Now, her dad drives a wheelchair,
unable to shift gears,
on wheels that take him to a bed
in his new home.

She sings those road songs to him now
and sits beside him in a passenger seat,
his life without memory
of all the first times.

And she hears his voice in the distance:
"There's not much time left;
we must go very slow."

How can I continue to give life meaning?

"After Life" by Leslie Lampe Long

"Viral Inspiration" by Dr. Stacy Berlin

River Guide

The viral inspiration …
the bloodbath,
immersed
in primitive expression
as I enter the river
with my guide,
the images
transforming to the moment
of my birth …
survival.
Lift, hold,
breathe.

After Life

Written in the early days of the pandemic when my fears evoked the experience of my cancer diagnosis

First the shock:
cancer, incurable.
Loss of self,
despair.
The search for lost twinship …
eventually
transformation,
acceptance,
existential living.
Dispelled fantasies
of immortality.
Gratitude,
a survived self,
hope.

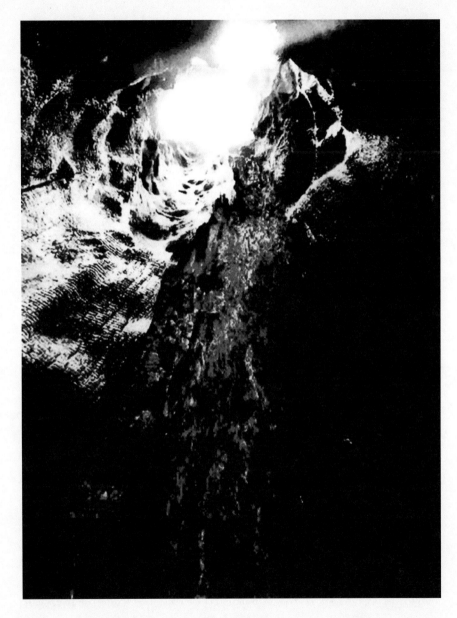

"A Glow of Moonlight" by Dan & Karen Busch

Taken the summer before my brother-in-law was rendered paraplegic after being crushed from behind by an ATV in the Nevada Hills

Resilience

Dedicated to my sister

Vegas

No past regrets,
no future worry,
only what is—
supercharged.
What happens here stays.

Play Interrupted

A speeding sledge
hammers from behind;
suddenly motionless,
time stops,
mortality looms.

Life Upside Down

Mechanical breaths,
pinned immobile
but no surrender.
Will they ever be the same?
Her true love healing,
living upside down.

New Light

The symbols,
adapted wheels,
adapted access.
The reality,
transformation.
On the road
driven by what can be
to bring them safely home.

Beyond Vegas

No past regrets,
no future worry;
what happens only here,
their true life beyond.

What Is a Hero?

New vitality, new dreams,
survival of spirit,
love stronger than loss.

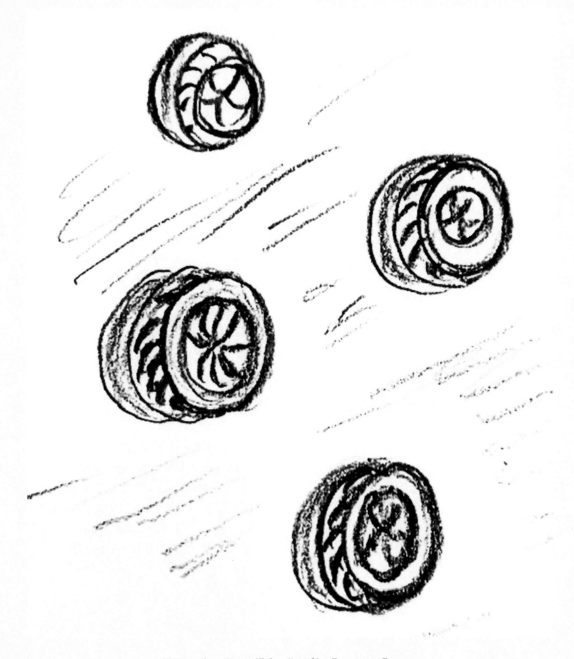

"On the Road" by Leslie Lampe Long

Licensed

16

Free and fresh behind the wheels,
a follower belonging
to the rules.
Within the lines—stay.
The weight of freedom,
tests my "good girl" self,
rattles keys
and opens a door to the world.
How do I belong now?
Following, turning, returning,
unknowing,
the risky wrong turn …
all eyes on this "good" girl.
New rules, the weight of freedom,
not knowing
but permitted …
my voice rattles,
my father, my teacher.

70

Many wheels now,
the long and winding road,
past expectations.
All too much, knowing
and not knowing,
obstacles, detours,
so much loss.
Asking then,
invisible now,
new rules … the lines of life,
a weightless gratitude.
Belonging now
to my legacy—
the lightness of leaving
regrets behind,
and when I ask,
my mother forgives.

When we open our eyes, what do we see?

When we reach out, who is there?

Can we see what others fail to see?

When we open our hearts, what do we feel?

Can we continue to give life meaning?

"CO-CREATING," by Leslie Lampe Long

Printed in the United States
by Baker & Taylor Publisher Services